Orcas

Victoria Blakemore

Copyright info/picture credits

Cover, Tory Kallman/Shutterstock; Page 3, ivkovich/AdpbeStock; Page 5, Rocky Grimes/AdobeStock; Page 7, Mrs-Brown/Pixabay; Page 9, MindfulChar/Pixabay; Pages 10-11, mur162/AdobeStock; Page 13, Andrea Izzotti/AdobeStock; Page 15, elvis santana/AdobeStock; Page 17, RKP/AdobeStock; Page 19, skampixelle/AdobeStock; Page 21, jamiessg/Pixabay; Page 23; pr2is/AdobeStock; Page 25, skeeze/Pixabay; Page 27, Tory Kallman/Shutterstock; Page 29, eldeiv/AdobeStock; Page 31, skeeze/Pixabay; Page 33, gruecolant/AdobeStock; Page 35, Andreas Edelmann/AdobeStock

Table of Contents

What Are Orcas?

Orcas are the largest members of the dolphin family. Like other members of the dolphin family, they are mammals.

Orcas are also known as killer whales or blackfish.

Coloration

Most of an orca's body is black. They have white spots behind their eyes. Their belly and the bottom of their tail is also white.

They have a gray patch behind their **dorsal fin**.

Orcas may use their coloration as **camouflage**. When light hits them in the water, they can be hard for prey to see.

Physical Characteristics

Orcas have a very round body that narrows at their head and tail. Their **streamlined** shape helps them to swim fast.

They also have powerful tail fins. Their tail fins, or flukes, help to **propel** them.

They have a tall **dorsal fin** that helps them **maintain** their body temperature.

Habitat

Most orcas are found in cold waters. They have thick layers of **blubber** under their skin. It allows them to stay warm in cold water.

There are some orcas that prefer the warmer tropical waters.

Range

Orcas can be found in all four oceans. Most are found in the Arctic and Pacific oceans.

Orcas may follow the **migration** of their prey. They do not migrate like many other marine mammals.

Diet

Orcas are **carnivores**, which means that they eat only meat.

Their diet is made up of seals, sea lions, fish, birds, and whales. They have also been known to eat sharks.

Some orcas swim up onto the beach to catch prey. This is called beaching. It is dangerous because they could get stuck on land.

Orcas are great hunters.

They work as a team to herd

fish to one area and

surround them.

Then, they take turns

swimming through the fish

and catching them.

Orcas can use their powerful tail to fan the water. This can help move fish into a group.

Communication

Orcas use sounds to communicate with each other. They make sounds like squeaks, clicks, whistles, and pops.

Each orca sounds a bit different. They can tell each other apart from far away by sound.

Different groups of orcas

make different sounds.

Echolocation

Orcas use something called

echolocation to find their way

and look for food.

Echolocation is when an

animal makes a clicking sound

and listens for it to bounce off

of objects. Orcas use that

echo to know where things

are.

Echolocation helps orcas when it is too dark for them to see very well.

Movement

Orcas usually swim at speeds of about four miles per hour. When hunting, they may swim up to forty miles per hour in short bursts.

They need to come to the surface to breathe. They do this using the blowhole on top of their head.

Orcas often breach, or leap out

of the water. Scientists think it

may be to shake **parasites** off

of their skin.

21

Pod Life

A group of orcas is called a pod. It is often made up of between five and thirty orcas.

Pods are usually a family group. They travel and hunt together.

Orcas have very close bonds

with their pod.

Orca Calves

Orcas have one calf. Once a calf is born, it will stay with it's mother for two or more years.

Female orcas work together to help mothers take care of calves.

After a few years, calves can join the other orcas in hunting and caring for young.

Life Span

In the wild, orcas often live between thirty and fifty years. Females tend to live longer than males.

Some orcas may live past eighty. It depends on how healthy the orca is and how much food is available.

Theme Parks

Some orcas are kept in theme parks and aquariums. They may perform in shows for people to watch.

They are also studied by scientists so that we can learn more about them.

Many people think that orcas

should not be kept at

aquariums or perform in shows.

Population

Researchers are not sure how many orcas there are in the wild. They think there are around 50,000.

The only kind of orca that is **endangered** is the southern resident killer whale. They are found in the Pacific ocean.

In 2016, there were only 78

southern resident killer whales

left in the wild.

Helping Orcas

Orca populations may be in trouble in the future.

Pollution from man-made chemicals can make orcas sick. **Overfishing** by humans has made it harder for some orcas to find food.

Laws have been passed to try to protect orca populations.

Many groups are also trying to help protect orcas. They are trying to stop pollution, **overfishing**, and hunting of orcas.

People want to protect orcas

and keep them from

becoming **endangered**.

Glossary

Blubber: fat that keeps animals warm

Camouflage: using color to blend in to the surroundings

Carnivore: an animal that eats meat.

Dorsal fin: the large fin on top of orcas

Endangered: at risk of becoming extinct

Maintain: keep the same

Migration: traveling from one

place to another

Overfishing: catching too

many fish

Parasites: plant or animal that

lives on other living things

Propel: push forward

Streamlined: smooth, rounded

surface that allows for fast

movement through water

About the Author

Victoria Blakemore is a first grade

teacher in Southwest Florida with a

passion for reading.

You can visit her at

www.elementaryexplorers.com

Also in This Series

Gray Wolves	**Sloths**	**Flamingos**	**Camels**	**Koalas**	**Honey Bees**
Pandas	**Pangolins**	**White-Tailed Deer**	**Orcas**	**Giraffes**	**Corn**
Meerkats	**Echidnas**	**Walruses**	**Raccoons**	**Bald Eagles**	**Apples**
Arctic Foxes	**Red Pandas**	**Cassowaries**	**Tigers**	**Ladybugs**	**Moose**
Beluga Whales	**Leopards**	**Elephants**	**Jellyfish**	**Binturongs**	**Lions**
Dolphins	**Reindeer**	**Hammerhead Sharks**	**Hippos**	**Pumpkins**	**Peafowl**

Elementary Explorers

Victoria Blakemore

Also in This Series

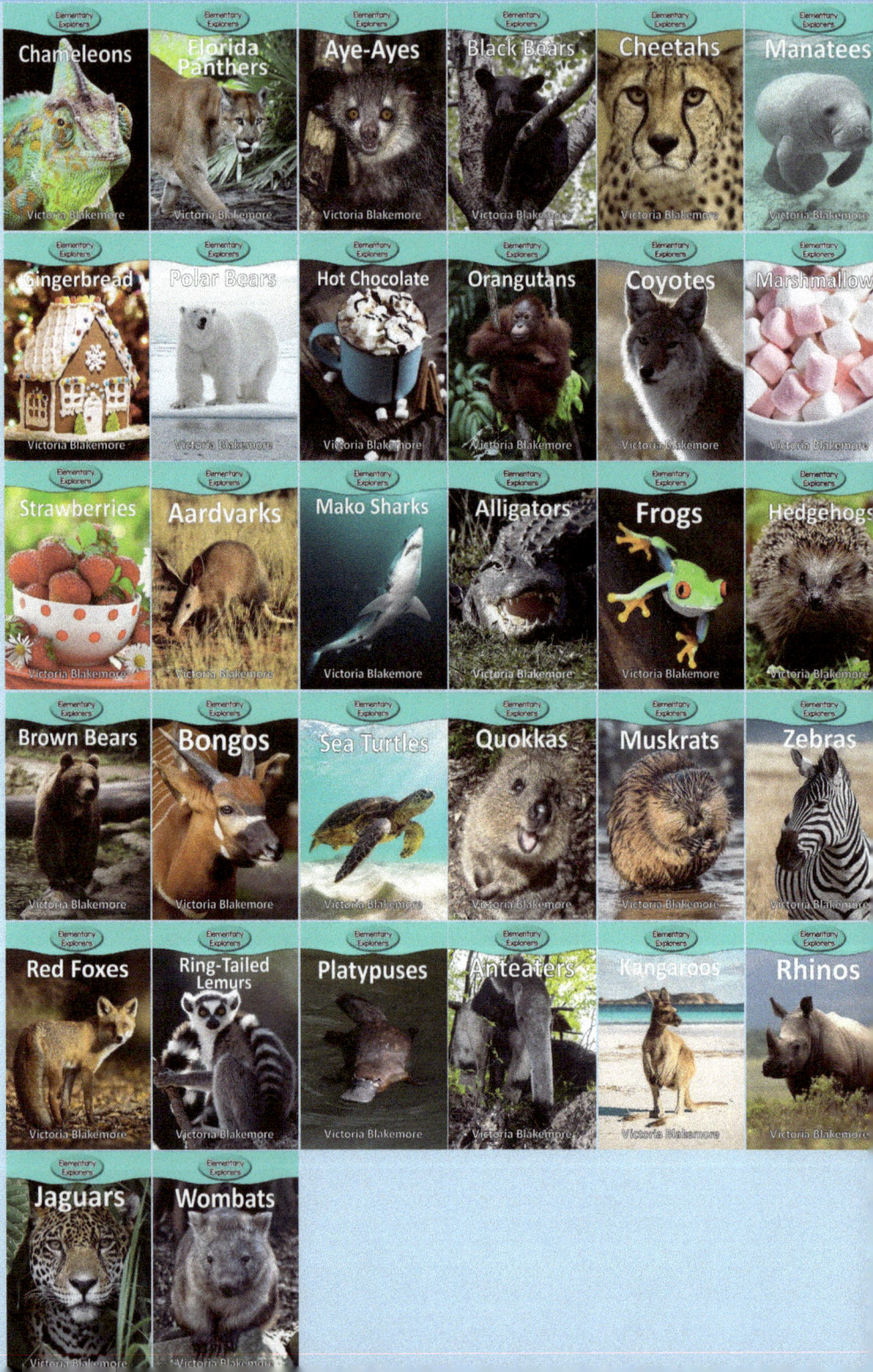

Chameleons	Florida Panthers	Aye-Ayes	Black Bears	Cheetahs	Manatees
Gingerbread	Polar Bears	Hot Chocolate	Orangutans	Coyotes	Marshmallow
Strawberries	Aardvarks	Mako Sharks	Alligators	Frogs	Hedgehogs
Brown Bears	Bongos	Sea Turtles	Quokkas	Muskrats	Zebras
Red Foxes	Ring-Tailed Lemurs	Platypuses	Anteaters	Kangaroos	Rhinos
Jaguars	Wombats				

All books by Victoria Blakemore, Elementary Explorers series.

www.ingramcontent.com/pod-product-compliance
Lightning Source LLC
Chambersburg PA
CBHW051250020426
42333CB00025B/3139